Sins of th[||||||||]ty

THE REAL LOS ANGELES NOIR

JIM HEIMANN

CHRONICLE BOOKS
SAN FRANCISCO

Thanks go out to all of those folks who made puttin[g]
this book together as uneventful as possible. I am esp[e]
cially indebted to several individuals who allowed me
access to their collections and who generously assiste[d]
in my research. Inspiration for this compilation goes t[o]
Dace Taube of the Regional History Center at the
University of Southern California. By allowing me the
freedom to spend hours poring over the Center's co[l]
lection, a concept evolved that was the seed for Sins [of]
the City. The generosity of the Williams family—Dino
Greg, and Alexa—and the unselfish access to their co[l]
lection was also instrumental in cementing my propo[sal]
and completing this book. Carolyn Cole of the Los
Angeles Public Library History Department Photo
Collections continues to be a driving force in the
preservation of Los Angeles' visual history, and her
insight and help in this project were invaluable. There
are always a handful of people who never hesitate t[o]
help me out when a request for images goes out. To
Brad Benedict, Michael Dawson, Bruce Henstell, Mar[k]
Wanamaker, Delmar Watson, and Tom Zimmerman a
heartfelt thanks. A hearty handshake goes to Glenn
Parsons for his patience and great job in creating an
appropriate cover design for a complex book. On th[e]
technical end of things, digital master Tina Thomas o[nce]
again contributed the time and expertise necessary t[o]
construct a project with tight deadlines and countles[s]
revisions. At Chronicle, my editor, Alan Rapp, was the
kingpin in seeing this project succeed, and his extra
attention to its complexities are greatly appreciated.
Additional credit goes to Anne Galperin who kept th[e]
design process and production on course and on tim[e]
And finally to Roleen and Zoë for being there.

Excerpt from Incredible Land by Basil Woon, with
illustrations by Wynn Holcomb, copyright © 1933 and
renewed © 1960 by Basil Woon. Reprinted with
permission of Liveright Publishing Corporation. Excer[pt]
from Miss Lonelyhearts and The Day of the Locust,
copyright © 1939 by Estate of Nathanael West.
Reprinted by permission of New Directions Publishin[g]
Corporation. Excerpts from The Big Sleep, copyright
© 1939 by Raymond Chandler and renewed © 1966
by Mrs. Helga Greene; Farewell, My Lovely, copyright
© 1940 by Raymond Chandler and renewed © 1967
by Mrs. Helga Greene; The High Window, copyright
© 1942 by Raymond Chandler and renewed © 1969
by Mrs. Helga Greene. Reprinted with permission of
Vintage Books, a division of Random House. Excerpt
from Ask the Dust, copyright © 1939, 1980 by John Fa[nte]
Reprinted with permission of Black Sparrow Press.
Excerpt from The Simple Art of Murder, copyright
© 1934, 1935, 1936, 1938, 1939, 1944, 1950 by Raymond
Chandler. Copyright © 1939 The Curtis Publishing
Company. The stories in The Simple Art of Murder
appeared in a Houghton Mifflin Company book, 1950
Reprinted with permission of Houghton Mifflin
Company. Excerpt from After Many a Summer Dies t[he]
Swan, copyright © 1939, 1976 by Aldous Leonard Hux[ley]
Reprinted with permission of the American Reprint
Company.

Library of Congress Cataloging-in-Publication Data
available.

ISBN 0-8118-2319-9

Printed in Hong Kong.

Distributed in Canada by Raincoast Books
8680 Cambie Street, Vancouver,
British Columbia V6P 6M9

Book Design by Jim Heimann

Cover Design by Glenn Parsons

Digital Composition by Tina Thomas

10 9 8 7 6 5 4 3 2 1

Chronicle Books
85 Second Street
San Francisco, California 94105

www.chroniclebooks.com

Sins of the City

TABLE OF CONTENTS

LOS ANGELES. CITY OF THE ANGELS. HOME TO HOLLYWOOD, PALM TREES, AND ENDLESS ROWS OF ORANGE GROVES. THE GLOWING AND GLOSSY IMAGE THAT WAS SOLD TO THE WORLD BY THE CHAMBER OF COMMERCE FOR OVER A CENTURY DEFTLY HID THE CITY'S UNDERBELLY, A SECRET VIEW VIVID AND RIPE AS THE SLICK PROMOTIONAL PROPAGANDA.

Both sides of L.A. views were documented in the precise pictures taken by the city's commercial and newspaper photographers. Photographs from the twenties through the fifties portray a changing landscape of altered streets, leveled hills, and destroyed buildings. Photos detail the nightclubs and bars, the buried bodies, the lifeless forms on coroners' slabs, Hollywood celebrities, boulevard degenerates, and self-proclaimed saviors of the soul. The images expose the bright and the dark side of a city absorbed in the present and looking toward the future. They document a city in constant change, rapidly evolving from adobe squalor to "The Wonder City of the West."

Photographers could make the town look good and bad. The glamour shots helped bring thousands of transplants to the Southland. Pictures of mountains, sun, and surf promised a better life and unlimited possibilities. But newspaper and tabloid photos showed newcomers that the seductive vision wasn't necessarily true. The flip side of paradise was a different Southland, a web of dope rings, petty criminals, sensational murders, ladies of the evening, bullet-riddled bodies, and a notoriously corrupt police force. It was the other L.A., a city awash in corruption and sin. Posed and candid. The good and the bad. A city to aspire to and a city to revile. Both versions were responsible for creating the mythic City of the Angels. The photos and stories told of a town on the backslide, documented in black and white, furnishing the reality behind the writer's fiction.

The Los Angeles that most of these early noir writers found was unlike anyplace they had been. There was the physical beauty of mountains, beaches, and agricultural plains within earshot of slums and urban glut. A polyglot of races walked the sidewalks. The architecture was bizarre, borrowed, or modern beyond a Midwesterner's imagination. There was Filmland imagined and real. Hollywood and Vine, mansions, movie premieres, nightspots, and studio fences obscured the fantasy. There were celebrities, crackpots, cults, and cemeteries for burying your pets. Floods, fire, and earthquakes reminded residents nothing was permanent here. There was a lack of history, but also the chance to leave everything behind—to experiment and reinvent. And there was crime. Just like any other city. But here everything seemed larger than life and just a bit skewed. Prostitution, gambling, and drugs provided a livelihood for thugs as well as cops. Both factions served as enforcers. All of this filtered through pen and paper, and later celluloid, to become L.A. noir.

Almost from the start, Los Angeles had a reputation as a hell-hole. In the mid-1800s it was filled with murderers, vigilantes, thieves, and prostitutes. Streets were rutted paths where mongrel dogs roamed and dead animals were dumped. L.A.'s first notoriety in national headlines was spurred by the massacre of Chinese immigrants near the old city plaza on the Calle de los Negros. Commonly known in those days as "nigger alley," it was described in Morrow Mayo's book *Los Angeles,* as "a dreadful thoroughfare, forty feet wide, running one whole block, filled entirely with saloons, gambling-houses, dance halls and cribs. It was crowded night and day with people of many races, male and female, all rushing and crowding along from one joint to another....Nigger Alley was a madhouse, filled with a mass of drunken, crazy Indians, of all ages, fighting, dancing, killing each other off with knives and clubs, and falling paralyzed drunk in the street. Every weekend three or four were murdered."

In 1871 this crowd went on a killing spree after a Chinese resident, shooting wildly in the street, accidentally hit "a white man." Within minutes denizens of the area swarmed the Chinese enclave, lynching, ransacking, stabbing, and beating "the heathens." Eventually nineteen victims were left dead. The Grand Jury indicted one hundred and fifty men, with six sent to jail. Several days later the six were released on a technicality. A pattern was set. It was no wonder the city was given the cynical sobriquet

Living on the fault line. Collapsed buildings from the Long Beach earthquake of 1933.

"Los Diablos" by newspapers throughout the country.

Things changed as the century turned. But not much. Corrupt city government and a police force of dubious reputation greeted masses of freshly arrived and gullible newcomers who flocked to the "Athens of the West." Many transplants found plenty of sunshine but not much else. Water, a key ingredient that was brought to the Southland under questionable circumstances and made millions for a privileged few, had, in a matter of years, transformed a desert into a mock Eden of imported vegetation and made-up architecture. Fortunes were made on oil and land, scandals ensued, and graft and petty crime became part of the picture. The population rush brought out the scam artists, fakes, frauds, and nut cases who joined the parade and were quick to take advantage of the situation. To fill psychic and real voids, many newcomers joined clubs for the lonesome or sought solace in the healers of the soul, evangelists who rushed to assuage the lost sheep with calls for prayer and money.

In the early part of the twentieth century, L.A. seemed like many other large American cities—corruption and vice came with urban territory. What made L.A. different was newness, geography, the car, and Hollywood. The car made a big difference. Other cities had developed around traditional horse-drawn vehicles or railroads, and their growth was usually hard, steady, and limited. Los Angeles was a twentieth-century city and the first metropolis to come of age with the automobile as its primary means of transportation. With four hundred and fifty square miles of roads, L.A. had plenty of room and the city boomed. Hollywood was part of that boom. The mere mention of its name made headlines blossom quicker than in any other city in the world. Hollywood set itself apart from the rest of the world and made everything seem larger than life. It was an easy mark, and a seemingly

ceaseless fountain of inspiration for writers.

In the 1920s prohibition increased the problems. A dry city had to be supplied, and plenty of hoodlums bribed the local law enforcers to place a case or keg into the right hands. Culver City, "the Heart of Screenland," was a case in point. It was home to M.G.M., Hal Roach, Ince, and a host of other studios, and its main drag, Washington Boulevard, was a hotbed of speakeasies, gin joints, roadhouses, and cafes—a precursor to the famed Sunset Strip. Film money and the town's "open" reputation brought the crowds to back rooms filled with gambling, bookmaking, and prostitution. The city soon built a race track, boxing ring, and a dog racing arena, all magnets for hoodlums. With direct access to rumrunners and local stills, the town was afloat in illegal booze. The Culver police force was notorious for looking the other way, losing evidence, and bungling raids, so life and crime went on undisturbed.

Culver City wasn't alone. Vernon, Venice, and the rest of Southern California seemed to have an unquenchable thirst for liquor, vice, and corruption. And you could always count on Hollywood to make national headlines. The film industry, firmly entrenched by the 1920s, provided more than enough money for the movie colonies' excesses. A series of scandals early in the decade finally brought to the front page what had been simmering for years behind closed doors: Fatty Arbuckle's alleged rape and murder of Virginia Rappe, the drug-related death of Wallace Reid, and the murder and questionable sexual orientation of William Desmond Taylor gave the public a ringside seat to Hollywood. Orgies, hoodlums, ignominious death—Hollywood had it all.

Gangs and crime bosses knew a good thing when they sniffed it and came crawling across the country to set up shop. Bootleggers such as Tony Cornero,

Dominic DiCiolla, and Albert Marco, controlled the business. Vice lords Guy McAfee, Nola Hahn, Jack Dragna, and Bob Gans commandeered their turf, laying claim to numbers rackets, prostitution, gambling, and slot machines. They were local hoodlums and they liked it that way. In return for a bit of profit sharing, the local law enforcers were expected to protect them from East Coast concerns muscling in on their territory. When Al Capone came calling in 1927, he was met by a couple of detectives and a vocal chief of detectives who made it clear that the welcome mat wasn't out. Rumor had it Capone was scouting a sea coast ranch to serve as a drop point for Canadian liquor. After a visit by the cops, he headed back to Chicago, ending his California "vacation." It would be a few more years until real East Coast muscle dropped anchor in the City of the Angels.

The cops could be counted on for more than just keeping East Coast gangsters at bay. The kingpin of police corruption was chief of police Ed "Two Gun" Davis. He and his city-hall cronies made sure L.A. remained safe for bribes and graft, which escalated in

the twenties and thirties to a wholesale spoils system. Their regime culminated in 1938 with the car bombing of private investigator Harry Raymond, an ex-LAPD detective who was in the process of exposing the corruption. The bombers were traced back to LAPD's Intelligence Squad, and the ensuing public outrage ousted Mayor Frank Shaw, while Chief Davis, along with twenty-three of his fellow officers, was forced into resigning.

One of L.A.'s important contributions to the regular rackets lay three miles off its coast. The first gambling ship arrived in 1928 to entertain and unload the pockets of residents and rubes. The various barges that anchored off the coast for the next decade were a lucrative trust for the local syndicate. Flaunting legal jurisdiction, they operated openly until the late thirties, when a series of raids finally grounded them. Ships such as the *Rex*, the *Montfalcone*, the *Tango*, and the *Monte Carlo* were memorably drafted onto the pages of Raymond Chandler's *The Big Sleep*.

Los Angeles was also hit with sensational crimes. The case of Edward Hickman and the kidnapping and dismemberment of twelve-year-old Marion Parker in

A stretch of Ventura Boulevard in Studio City disappears under the annual ravages of winter flooding, ca. 1938.

December of 1927 filled headlines for days. Likewise, in 1929, jailed suspects Jack Hawkins and his pal "Zeke" Hayes created a stir with their gun battle with the police within the courthouse elevator. The two had a long record, including the alleged torture and killing of a San Francisco cop, and Hawkins was set up for a taste of swift L.A. sheriff–style justice.

Los Angeles' growing unsavory reputation gave the pulpit pounders plenty to sermonize about. To the newly arrived who flocked in droves to hear and see them, evangelists and preachers such as Aimee Semple McPherson and "Fighting Bob" Shuler offered the healing balm of acceptance and security for lost souls—as long as the collection plate was full.

Occasionally, as in the case of Reverend Shuler, their investigations into civic affairs exposed the graft that had become an indelible part of the city. Going after perceived and real moral enemies, the preachers sometimes actually helped to reform temporarily the tarnished city. Their antics were used for atmosphere in several L.A. films and novels. In *The Day of the Locust*, Nathanael West lampooned these religious aberrations: "He spent his nights at the different Hollywood churches, drawing the worshipers. He visited the 'Church of Christ, Physical' where holiness was attained through the constant use of chest-weights and spring grips; the 'Church Invisible' where fortunes were told and the dead made to find lost objects; the 'Tabernacle of the Third Coming' where a women in male clothing preached the 'Crusade Against Salt'; and the 'Temple Moderne' under whose glass and chromium roof 'Brain-Breathing, the Secret of the Aztecs' was taught."

L.A.'s eccentric side was punctuated by other cult leaders. The Church of I Am was started by a husband and wife team, Guy and Edna Ballard, who hit town in 1932 and immediately started pedaling their new reli-

gion that was based on St. Germain, a murky deity who supposedly gave off a violet ray of supernatural powers. The Ballards accepted "love offers" for their preaching efforts. At their temple near downtown L.A., topped by a blazing "I Am" neon sign, as many as ten thousand worshipers were also sold products such as "New Age cold cream" and "Flame In Action" electronic devices. Their son, Donald, claimed he had an invisible power, derived from ascended spirits and called K-17, that was so powerful it had sunk several Nazi submarines. The Ballards were eventually prosecuted for mail fraud, but by the time the charges were overturned, the steam had run out of the cult and the guileless and gullible moved on to new saviors.

The thirties saw L.A. expanding. The disjointed communities that had spread over the plain began to congeal into a mass of endless streets. Newcomers arrived daily. Potential stars, "Okies" looking for work, the displaced, and dreamseekers filled the apartments, bungalows, and skid rows.

This constantly evolving city proved irresistible for local writers, who observed and translated what they saw around them into vivid passages that contrasted the physical beauty with the gaudiness. Even the architecture cooperated. Oddball buildings in the shape of toads, pigs, and frogs were passed off as a common cityscape, and while it was true that Los Angeles supported the avante garde in architecture, more common were low-slung buildings and bungalows. Aldous Huxley in *After Many a Summer Dies the Swan* described such a landscape in a mid-thirties drive from downtown:

> Then suddenly the car plunged into a tunnel
> and emerged into another world, a vast, untidy,
> suburban world of filling stations and bill-
> boards, of low houses in gardens, of vacant lots

and waste paper, of occasional shops and office buildings and churches—primitive Methodist churches built, surprisingly enough, in the style of the Cartuja at Granada, Catholic churches like Cantebury Cathedral, synagogues disguised like the Hagia Sophia, Christian Science churches with pillars and pediments. . . . The car was traveling westwards and the sunshine, slanting from behind them as they advanced, lit up each building, each sky sign and billboard as though with a spotlight, as though on purpose to show the new arrivals all the sights. Eats. Cocktails. Open nites. Jumbo Malts. Do Things, Go Places With Consol Super-Gas!. . .The car sped onwards, and here in the middle of a vacant lot was a restaurant in the form of a seated bulldog, the entrance between the front paws, the eyes illuminated. . . . Classy Eats. Mile High Cones. Jesus Saves. Hamburgers. Astrology. Numerology. Psychic Readings. Drive In For Nutburgers.

Hollywood continued to fulfill fantasies. Yet shadows dimmed even the brightest aspects of movieland. Such was the case of film celebrity Thelma Todd, who was murdered in 1935. Though plenty of theories and suspects have been disclosed, her death remains unsolved. Combining all of the classic elements—hoods, gambling, and a fur-clad corpse slumped over the steering wheel of a car in an exhaust-filled garage—Thelma Todd's case could only have happened in filmdom's nether world.

Not film related, but just as dark and sensational, was the bizarre story of "The Rattlesnake Murderer." Robert James loved women, kinky sex, and taking out insurance policies. His case may have been inspirational, in part, for James Cain's novel *Double Indemnity.*

The reality of the James crime was, however, much darker. A transplant to Los Angeles, James had left a dead wife or two with substantial life insurance policies behind him before settling down in La Cañada. He opened a downtown barbershop and developed a noisy (by neighbors' accounts) sadomasochistic love-making style with his newly insured wife. When funds began running low, he killed his spouse by thrusting her foot in a box containing two rattlesnakes.

Nineteen thirty-eight was a turning point in Los Angeles crime annals. The bombing of private investigator Harry Raymond's car and the ensuing investigation had exposed corruption in the police force and among city officials. Mayor Frank Shaw was implicated and he was eventually replaced by reformist Fletcher Bowron. Raids increased on nightspots, gambling joints, and other sources of vice. Feeling the heat and having lost their close political ties, some of the era's top crime bosses headed out of town to Las Vegas.

While this clean-up signaled the end of one era, much crime and police corruption lingered into the next decades. As the Second World War loomed, officials paid attention to eliminating graft. War reporting replaced the sensational crime headlines. But the war also exposed darker problems involving the black market, gangs, and mobsters such as Mickey Cohen. Acknowledged as a loud-mouthed thug, Cohen was one of the city's splashiest underworld characters. Attracted to vice in all its forms, he dressed the part, hung out at all the right places, and made enemies with all the wrong people. Constantly in the news, he was trailed by the LAPD and Sheriff's Department, who busted him periodically for small-time infractions that eventually led to larger crimes. Several attempts on his life by rivals kept Mickey moving, but not fast enough for the local cops and Feds, who eventually put him behind bars for fifteen years on tax evasion charges.

Hollywood, too, changed. After the war, the star system and the stranglehold the studios held on their stars' lives began to disintegrate. Studios faced increased competition and began to lose their influence on the public. Postwar movies reflected this different mood in the pronounced pessimism of the noir films that were created during this period. The rise of Las Vegas after the war emptied many of the nightspots of top-name talent, leaving a vacuum in L.A.'s entertainment scene. Small hip joints became increasingly popular. The essence of hip and cool, they prospered on main drags and side streets all over the town. Joining them were a few prime clubs such as Ciro's, Mocambo, and the Crescendo on Sunset Boulevard. The criminals backing many clubs on "The Strip" heightened the street's tawdry allure.

One district that matched Sunset's popularity was in the heart of L.A.'s Black community. Central Avenue, in L.A.'s "Darktown," was a hotbed of juke joints, jazz clubs, and glorified seediness. Its reputation as ground zero for music and drugs drew cops trying to keep things in check. Whites and celebs went there "slumming" for authentic jazz and were seldom disappointed. Lining the corridor were the Apex (which begat the Club Alabam), the Downbeat, the Last Word, Club Memo, Dynamite Jackson's, Cafe Zombie, and the Plantation. Nearby were Ivie's Chicken Shack, the Barrelhouse, the Black Flamingo, and Cafe Society. In Little Tokyo (called "Bronzeville" during the war years when Blacks occupied the section vacated by local Japanese who had been interned) were the Cobra Club and Shep's Playhouse. The music scene and the pervasive hint of danger made "The Avenue" a prime destination for hipsters and an inspiration for writers.

In unincorporated parts of L.A. county, strip joints, burlesque halls, and card clubs also kept things rolling. Places such as Gardena, south of downtown

L.A., found loopholes in the law and set up legal gambling zones with a series of card clubs that gave local vice lords new territory. In the late forties, the Monterey Club, the Normandy, the Horseshoe, and others provided a mini Vegas-style strip where sanctioned illicit activity could simmer in relative obscurity. Likewise, beach front communities including Long Beach, Venice, and Santa Monica hosted "games of chance" that were just another form of illegal lottery. Bridgo, keno, tango, and bingo parlors were everywhere. These thinly veiled gambling dens fed small-time bunco artists for a short period after the war but were slowly eliminated by the mid-fifties.

Farther from the action but an indispensable part of the Los Angeles scene, Mexico was the perfect escape spot. Tijuana was conveniently close. It was a prime spot to hide out, score illegal drugs, partake in a bawdy strip show, or let all hell loose. For filmmakers, all the requisite noir atmosphere was present: Glaring and gaudy neon, mock-Spanish architecture, and the hint of impending danger in the dark, foul alleys and side streets.

Other locations surrounding L.A. served for assorted criminal activity. Palm Springs catered to its Hollywood contingent with members of the L.A. crime scene. The Dunes, a private gambling club run by Al and Lou Wertheimer, former Detroit mobsters, spiced up desert living with tuxedoed croupiers and lobster dinners. It was joined by the 139 Club, in less pretentious digs, but still offering its members games of chance. Up in the mountains, film celeb Noah Berry ran a guest resort that featured illegal booze and an isolated location that kept the cops at bay. In counties adjacent to L.A., cockfights, nudist colonies, and other assorted recreational offerings provided Angelenos with plenty of places to enjoy their vices. Beach villages up and down the coast were favored as rendezvous for those wanting to escape the scrutiny of cops and photographers.

After World War II, L.A. lost enough low-grade crime to keep corruption at a respectable level. The sex trade always operated. In the late forties Brenda Allen, one of L.A.'s most prominent madams, faced a series of raids at her rented house of ill-repute. The case escalated into a full scale scandal when it was discovered that a member of the vice squad was cozy with Brenda and hush money was changing hands to keep the house of pleasure open. Other police officers were implicated, and a healthy batch of movie colony stars and executives were listed in Brenda's "little black book." The whole affair got so complicated that eventually, like many vice cases in L.A., nothing much happened. Brenda was finally thrown in jail, the police chief resigned, and the cops in question were demoted.

In the hills and flatlands of L.A., the homosexual community had a group of nightspots and pick up locations that were subjected to endless raids. In the early thirties "The Barn," a club on Cahuenga just south of Sunset, was raided for offering a revue of "pansies," men donning women's clothes. "The Run," a stretch of 5th Street near downtown L.A.'s skid row, was a notorious pick-up area. In South Central L.A., flamboyant drag shows, first organized in the early thirties and presented at places such as the Club Alabam and Jack's Bird In A Basket, played to a large and active homosexual society in the Black community.

Back in Hollywood, the Café Gala, sequestered on an embankment above Sunset, was a popular supper club that offered movieland sophisticates a chance to listen to tunes played at dual grand pianos. Habitués of the club, which included a mix of top-notch Hollywood celebs, were not subjected to the raids that many of the other nameless "gay" clubs suffered at the hands of the LAPD, who summarily liked to nail "Hollywood deviants" for their unacceptable behavior.

Several unsolved headline crimes capped the end of the forties. A blast to the head of Bugsy Siegel on June 20, 1947, in girlfriend Virginia Hill's rented Beverly Hills house, ended the career of one of L.A.'s least camera shy figures. While speculation ran wild as to who bumped Bugsy, it was theorized that he had skimmed money from the construction of Las Vegas' Flamingo Hotel. Both his eyes were expertly hit by a sharpshooter, and the always dapper Benjamin Siegel's last photo op was on an unfashionable coroner's slab.

Just as mysterious, and even more grisly, was the murder and dismemberment of Elizabeth Short, whose bisected and blood-drained body was dumped in a vacant Crenshaw-area lot in January of 1947. Coined the *Black Dahlia* by newspaper copywriters, Betty Short was typical of the "girl coming to Hollywood seeking stardom." She tossed about in the nether world of Hollywood Boulevard, and her demise inspired several fictionalized accounts purporting to reveal her killer. Her murder remains on the LAPD's books as unsolved.

Caryl Chessman was a paroled robber and prison escapee who went on a crime spree that included robbing, raping, and kidnapping. Chessman preyed on several lovers lane couples who told police of being approached by a gunman using a red spotlight as a ruse to get them to open their windows. Thus Chessman received his nickname as the "Red-Light Bandit." After several weeks of mayhem, Chessman and an accomplice were spotted in east Hollywood, pursued, and taken into custody. Although Chessman alleged he was brutally beaten into confessing his involvement, he was sentenced to die for his seventeen convictions. For over a decade he stalled, acting in his own defense and receiving stays of execution. "The Red-Light Bandit" eventually lost his appeals and was executed in the gas chamber in 1960.

Former aviatrix Jeanne French was forty-five years

old when her battered nude body was discovered in a vacant lot on Grand View Boulevard in the Mar Vista section of L.A. Her homicide was quickly dubbed the "Red Lipstick" murder when her torso was discovered with an obscene inscription scrawled in lipstick and signed "B.D.—'Tex Andy.'" Police surmised the words were a cryptic reference to the Black Dahlia case which had occurred a month before. The search for the "werewolf slayer" initially included her ex-marine husband but ultimately the leads for her killer went nowhere, leaving this case another unsolved murder.

Marijuana, never a high-profile drug in pre-war L.A., got a boost in popularity when Robert Mitchum and a starlet were arrested for possession in a Laurel Canyon bungalow. Mitchum made tabloid fodder when his trial went public, but he hardly dented his bad boy image after serving his two-month sentence in county jail. It was a prime example of Hollywood justice.

Also in the fifties, "Sweater Girl" Lana Turner hooked up with Mickey Cohen cohort Johnny Stompanato. Their very public and torrid affair blazed even brighter when Lana's daughter, Cheryl Crane, (whose dad Stephen Crane owned a celeb haunt, the Luau restaurant in Beverly Hills), stabbed mom's suitor to death after Johnny got a little too rough with Miss Turner.

By the mid-fifties, L.A.'s noir reputation, both real and invented, was beginning to play itself out. Los Angeles was being boostered to death in unbridled optimism. The city was evolving and its dark side was beginning to look a little too bright and worn. The dozens of suburbs, forever in search of a city, were

congealing into an endless mass of concrete criss-crossed by freeways. Dispersment of the Southland's huge influx of post-war population flooded the virgin agricultural plains with cracker-box houses and shopping centers, moving nickel-and-dime crime to the suburbs. An emptying city center and the installation of a succession of new police chiefs diluted the free-range crime of previous decades. Real hoods high-tailed it to Vegas where murder and mayhem were a bit easier to commit. Many writers sensed this change and shifted their interest to other genres.

L.A.'s reputation for crime and corruption was enhanced with the creation of TV's *Dragnet*. The true escapades of L.A.'s underbelly, narrated in the spare tone of Sergeant Friday, was great fodder for the new medium, but the television hit failed to recreate the noir writers' descriptive nuances.

In the sixties, L.A. was no longer seen as a brooding and crime-infested metropolis. In fact, it seemed to be getting a bit homogenized. Contemporary writers such as James Ellroy, Walter Mosley, and several others would successfully recapture the head-pounding crime of bygone years, and films such as *Chinatown* and *L.A. Confidential* exposed the underlying evil of historic events. But the real L.A. noir, that black and blue vision of Los Angeles, where fast-talking dames and hardened detectives filled pulp pages and theater screens, had faded. Eventually, popular culture claimed it. What remains are the photographs that tell another story—a razor-sharp, singular, unfiltered documentation of the real pain and torture of a city grasping at adolescence, a Los Angeles full of pleasure and stained by sin.

A tarpaper shack and adjoining chicken coop are the site of a murder/suicide in the sticks outside of Los Angeles. Lancaster, 1944.

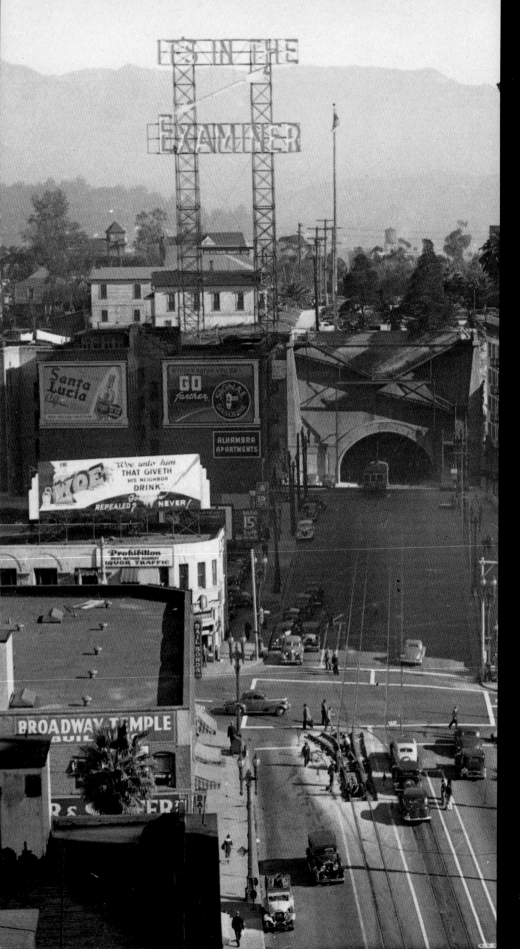

Opposite. City hall.
De facto symbol of
a city in sin.

MEAN STREETS

"DOWN THESE MEAN STREETS A MAN MUST GO
WHO HIMSELF IS NOT MEAN,
WHO IS NEITHER TARNISHED NOR AFRAID."

The Simple Art of Murder, Raymond Chandler

Transit point for the newly arrived and escapees from paradise: the Greyhound bus depot at 560 South Los Angeles Street, ca. 1939.

Straight off the bus, a Hollywood newcomer. Hollywood and Vine, ca. 1938.

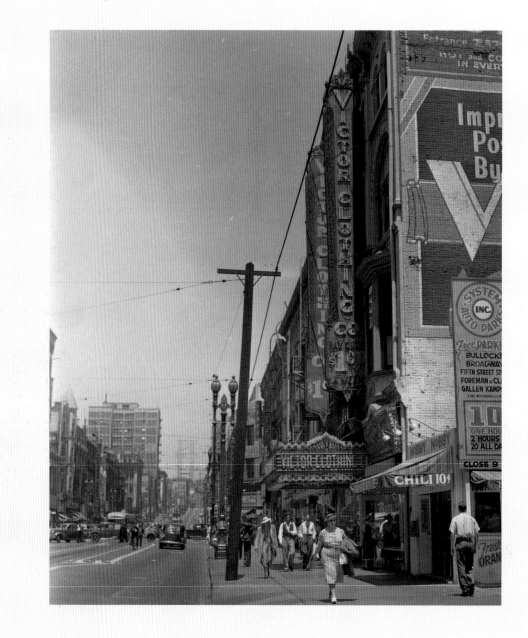

Downtown L.A.'s reputation as a magnet for crime was unsurpassed. It was a main source of inspiration for writers as well as location scouts who exploited palms, high rises, and Lysol-soaked alleys. Broadway looking north from 2nd Street, ca. 1936.

Behind even the most innocent-looking streets lurked a breeding ground for cheap thrills and illicit goods. Hill Street looking north from 2nd Street, ca. 1938.

"On Main Street are the pawnbrokers where you can buy a complete outfit for any outdoor labor—or, if you are poor and desperate, a gun. For those with the nickel or dime necessary there are dozens of cheap picture theaters, some of them showing silent horse-operas fully ten years old, and other pictures being made today which will certainly never reach *your* neighborhood theater."

Incredible Land, Basil Woon

Main Street, in the shadow of City Hall. Looking north with Union Station in the distance, ca. 1940.

"On and off Main Street, too, can be found the cheap brothels and speakeasies where fiery 'alky' is sold for as little as ten cents a gulp. One block west, on Spring, are the two financial centers— one legitimate stock exchange and the other the gamble and bootleg exchange where 'big shots' control the rum and roulette trade of Los Angeles."

Incredible Land, Basil Woon

Main Street tattoo parlor, a stock-in-trade business for the city's premiere sinister avenue, ca. 1943.

"On Main Street also are the Spanish language theaters and the burlesque theaters— the latter featuring 'strip acts' and pornographic language that would make Earl Carroll blush. Every once and a while a police censor visits one of these theaters, is properly shocked, and the next day the entire cast is carted off to jail, fined, admonished and then sent back to re-open the show."

Incredible Land, Basil Woon

The Follies, Main Street's well-attended burlesque hall.

Top. Snare drum, full orchestra, and a runway full of dames. **Bottom.** Backstage at the Follies.

Mile-high cones and jumbo malts. Currie's ice cream store in Beverly Hills opens with a film-style premiere, ca. 1936.

"The SunGold Market into which he turned was a large, brilliantly lit place. All the fixtures were chromium and the floors and walls were lined with white tile. Colored spotlights played on the showcases and counters, heightening the natural hues of the different foods. The oranges were bathed in red, the lemons in yellow, the fish in pale green, the steaks in rose, and the eggs in ivory."

The Day of the Locust, Nathanael West

Klieg lights greet customers to the opening of the Radio Center Market, 1334 Vine Street, Hollywood.

"I went up to my room, up the dusty stairs of Bunker Hill, past the soot-covered frame buildings along that dark street, sand and oil and grease choking the futile palm trees standing like dying prisoners, chained to a little plot of ground with black pavement hiding their feet."

Ask the Dust, John Fante

Burt Lancaster gets ready for the camera in front of a Bunker Hill flop house, the location for a scene in *Criss Cross*.

"Bunker Hill is old town, lost town, shabby town, crooktown. Once, a very long time ago, it was the choice residential district of the city, and there are still standing a few of the jigsaw Gothic mansions with wide porches and walls covered with round-end shingles and full corner bay-windows with spindle turrets. They are all rooming houses now, their parquet floors are scratched and worn through the once glossy finish and the wide sweeping staircases are dark with time and with cheap varnish laid over generations of dirt. In the tall rooms hagged landladies bicker with shifty tenants."

The High Window, Raymond Chandler

Bunker Hill, ca. 1939.

When the construction of Union Station, L.A.'s state-of-the-art rail depot, was announced in the mid-thirties, a displaced Chinatown was recreated with theme park undertones several blocks away, thinly veiling gambling and narcotics activity. **Top.** Entrance to New Chinatown, ca. 1938. **Bottom.** The back alleys of Chinatown, spawning ground of two-bit hoods and hookers.

Top. Japanese Fishing Village, Terminal Island. Home to a lucrative fishing fleet and suspected den of pre-war espionage activity, this enclave was effectively eliminated with the internment of the Japanese community after the attack on Pearl Harbor. **Bottom.** December 7, 1941. Cops patrol Little Tokyo seeking to calm nerves while keeping an eye out for suspicious activity.

Top. "Nutburgers" for sale on a stretch of what was to become "The Strip." Sunset Boulevard and Doheny, ca. 1934. **Bottom.** The Bungalow, a roadside restaurant, illustrates the rural atmosphere that would quickly become a victim of a growing metropolis. Sunset Boulevard at Sunset Plaza Drive, ca. 1934.

La Rue, Trocadero, Mocambo, and the Crillon. This cluster of high-style nightclubs on Sunset Strip was the core of a nocturnal playground for both stars and L.A.'s crime bosses.

Top. Exhibitionism and body worship. Hedonist pursuits practiced in earnest at Muscle Beach in nearby Santa Monica, a suburb favored as a location by fiction writers. **Bottom.** Malibu, a few miles up the coast from L.A., was the preferred beach resort for the movie colony. Secluded and smart, it was the perfect background for dark goings-on of the rich and corrupt denizens of nearby Los Angeles.

Top. Noah Beery's Paradise Trout Ranch, ca. 1931. The mountains of nearby Los Angeles could always be counted on as an escape from the city below. Lodges and clubs offered illicit pleasures such as gambling and prohibition booze. Film star Noah Beery created a rustic oasis that featured freshly caught trout served with slot machines and cocktails in Big Rock Canyon near the larger, more formal resorts of Big Bear and Arrowhead. The film crowd made it a frequent stop, and the fireplace boulders bore the autographs of the town's most celebrated players. Raymond Chandler, who frequented the area, may have found inspiration in this or similar resorts when he described a trek to a club in the outskirts of L.A. **Bottom.** Palm Springs, the desert resort several hours east of Los Angeles, was the polar opposite of coastal destinations. Hotels and dude ranches catered to the pampered needs of the rich and famous and, of course, scandal and crime were close by. The Dunes and 139 Club were two casinos in the pre-war period that provided blackjack, craps, and roulette courtesy of the Wertheimer brothers, associates of Detroit's Purple Gang.

If L.A. was a land of sin, Tijuana, across the Mexican border, was its unofficial capital. Narcotics, prostitutes, gambling, horse racing, pornography, divorces, and just about anything else were conveniently close. Hollywood celebs and L.A. gambling interests helped bring it to life, but by the 1950s their influence had dissipated, and T.J. had evolved into the essence of noir: dark, dangerous, and lethal. **Opposite.** Goldie, a popular stripper, does her stuff for American tourists looking for a good time. **Above.** Avenida Revolución, Tijuana's main drag, was wall-to-wall with strip joints, tourist traps, and suckers.

#p. 37

Detectives uncover the body of a murder victim buried in a bungalow garage, ca. 1932.

Dragging Echo Park Lake for a body, ca. 1935.

A cigar-chomping detective examines the murder weapon, a hatchet.

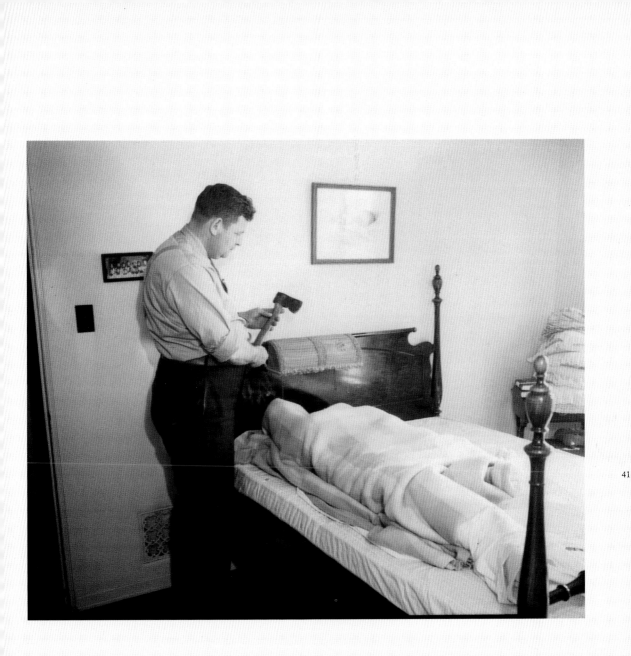

Wrapped in a sinister shroud, the victim of a hatchet murder reposes in bed minus one key body part.

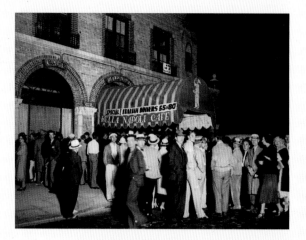

42

Top. Crowds gather at a gangland shooting in front of the Bella Napoli Cafe. 711 North Vermont. **Bottom.** Victims of the Bella Napoli shoot-out.

Violent end at an East L.A. juke joint.

Top. The Café Roost, 2700 West Temple Street. It was here that Les Bruneman, gang associate, was rubbed out as he sat with nurse-friend Miss Alice Ingram. Bruneman, who was arrested and acquitted for killing a cop, was about to open the Montmartre Cafe in Hollywood as a gambling place. He may have further speeded his demise when he complained to friends that "Reno dagoes" were out to get him, ca. October 1937. **Bottom.** Inside the Café Roost, Les Bruneman, with a shot to his head, awaits the coroner.

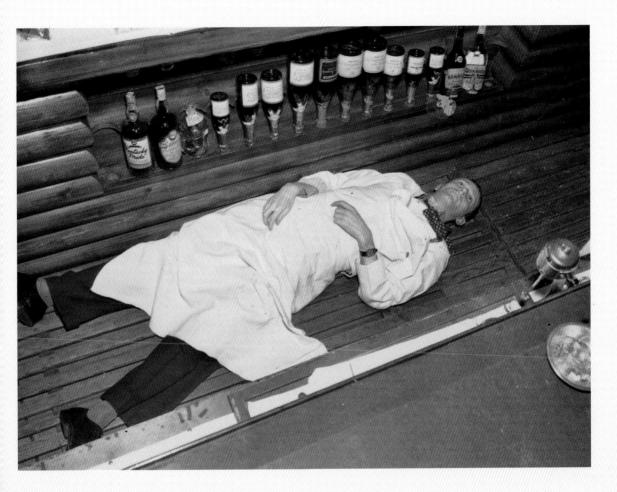

A bartender bites the dust in a Hollywood robbery gone awry, ca. 1940.

A typical L.A. landscape near downtown. Spring Street, before it was extended, trailed off into a dusty road, the perfect spot to abandon a body or smoke a reefer.

Detectives investigate an anonymous female victim, brutally sprawled out in one of the city's numerous vacant lots.

An LAPD crime team hunches over the corpse of a post–Black Dahlia murder case coined the "Lipstick Murder," ca. 1947.

Bleeding with a bullet in his body, a sturdy criminal is carted off to jail, ca 1954.

Above. Hollywood Division cops line up for their formal portrait, ca. 1930. **Opposite.** James Edgar "Two Gun" Davis, police chief during one of L.A.'s most notorious regimes, was a model of graft and internal police corruption. Under his alternating terms he established the "bum brigade" at the city's border to keep undesirables out of Depression-era L.A. and was finally "retired" after he was connected to the near-fatal bombing of an investigating reformer.

Unloading the Black Maria and bringing them in. Suspects cover their faces before newsmen can get their pictures, ca. 1950.

Part of the job, cops grill a suspect, ca. 1940.

The line-up. A typical weekly "showup" at a police station, ca. 1940.

Prisoners jammed in the city jail await justice, ca. 1945.

How to SIN in Hollywood

GLAMOURLAND

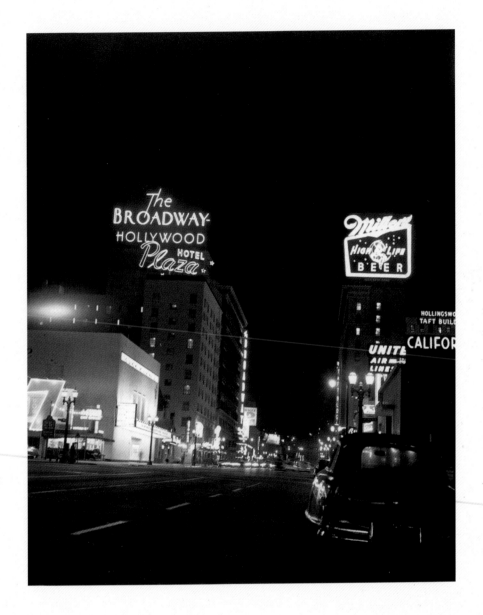

The famed Hollywood Brown Derby on Vine Street, celeb rendezvous, pre–prize fight
dinner joint, and nocturnal destination for both legit and underworld L.A. swells, ca. 1948.

59

Vine Street, looking north toward Hollywood Boulevard, was one of the city's premiere corridors. Jammed with jazz clubs, two-bit drink joints, radio studios, and high-end clothing stores, it became in the fifties a prime destination for the city's hipsters.

Tom Breneman's, in all its neon splendor, gives a taste of Vine Street glory, ca. 1941.

For serious nightclubbers, the sophisticated La Conga on Vine Street offered pricey entertainment and a chance to rub shoulders with the town's elite, ca. 1937.

NBC Studios at the corner of Sunset and Vine.

"When Todd reached the street, he saw a dozen great violet shafts of light moving across the evening sky in wide crazy sweeps. . . . The purpose of this display was to signal the world premiere of a new picture. . . . A young man with a portable microphone was describing the scene. His rapid, hysterical voice was like that of a revivalist preacher whipping his congregation toward the ecstasy of fits. 'What a crowd, folks! What a crowd! There must be ten thousand excited, screaming fans outside of Kahn's Persian tonight. The police can't hold them. Here, listen to them roar. . . . Did you hear it? It's a bedlam, folks. A veritable bedlam! What excitement! Of all the premières I've attended, this is the most . . . the most . . . stupendous, folks. Can the police hold them? Can they? It doesn't look so, folks . . .'"

The Day of the Locust, Nathanael West

A movie premiere at the Carthay Circle near Beverly Hills climaxed an evening in glamourland.

Above. The Cinegrill at the Hollywood Roosevelt. Top-name entertainers made it another hot spot for the cocktail and torch singers set, ca. 1938. **Opposite Top.** The Band Box, Fairfax Avenue. One of the many small clubs throughout Hollywood that harbored intimate surroundings for those in the know. The nightclub also served as a mail drop and after-hours meeting place for mobster Mickey Cohen and his associates, ca. 1940. **Opposite Bottom.** The interior of the Band Box was snug and casual. Signs throughout the club informed patrons to sample and mix their own "fancy" drinks. Impromptu performances by celebs were encouraged.

Top. Club 17 on Las Palmas Avenue where notables and underworld figures mingled. An illegal liquor payoff scandal resulted in a vice squad raid and headline news. A secret exit to Hollywood Boulevard provided customers with a quick escape route, October 1939. **Bottom.** Detectives bust patrons in an attempt to curb illegal gambling and after-hours drinking. Perennial raids were a veiled attempt by police to placate the public. The Casanova Club on the Strip, ca. 1941.

A typical scene of nightclub action in wartime Hollywood.

The Clover Club was private and for a reason. Only a select clientele was admitted to the club, which hovered above Sunset Boulevard at La Cienega, and Hollywood's high rollers were escorted to the backroom gaming tables guarded by machine gun–toting goons. Hollywood's elite could dump thousands in one evening in one of the towns most sophisticated set-ups.

Vice-squad detectives display $15,000 worth of confiscated gambling equipment after a pre-dawn Easter "blitzkrieg" at the Clover Club. The raid, with three hundred celebrities in attendance, also turned up $6,942 in cash. These periodic clampdowns eventually put the night spot out of business when gangland concerns found better pickings in Las Vegas, March 1940.

Hollywood's Famous Door, on the lower end of Vine Street, was the quintessential roadhouse within the city limits. A well-known celebrity hangout where stars and notables carved their autographs into the club's entry door.

The Haig, near the Wilshire Brown Derby and the Coconut Grove, was a hipster's paradise. All-night jam sessions by Gerry Mulligan and other top jazz performers made this the spot for "California Cool."

72

The Kings on Sunset Strip and the Hawaiian Paradise on Melrose Avenue had shadowy pedigrees.
Word was that both clubs had suspicious backers—a given for almost all of L.A.'s nightspots.

Top. Don the Beachcomber's on McCadden Place in Hollywood was one of the first clubs to exploit a tropical theme, making it a crowded venue for several decades. **Bottom.** Likewise for Stephen Crane's Luau in Beverly Hills, which saw a flurry of business after his daughter, Cheryl, was accused of killing Johnny Stompanato while she allegedly defended her mother, Lana Turner, from Stompanato's beatings.

The toast of Hollywood and hoodlums, Perino's Restaurant on Wilshire Boulevard, a celebrity establishment for L.A. blue bloods, also hosted assorted underworld figures who could afford the high-class atmosphere and prices.

Along with Ciro's and the Trocadero, Mocambo was ground zero for the toast of L.A. nightlife. Starting in the forties, it was *the* place to be seen and to see the cream of L.A.'s cabaret performers. Even after Las Vegas drew away some of the Sunset Strip's top talent, Mocambo could still pack 'em in.

Top. Bamba Club. A popular destination for slumming thrill seekers, this seedy downtown nightclub was a good place to score more than just dames and beer. Located in the Mexican section of town, its noir atmosphere was incorporated into the filming of *Criss Cross*. North Main Street, ca. 1947. **Bottom.** A long-running and successful club on Beverly Boulevard, the Bar of Music was a cozy spot for intimate chat and prolonged cocktails. Off the beaten path, the nightspot featured top cabaret entertainment and harbored a reputation as a hangout for hipsters and underworld types.

Bouncer "Cairo Mary" ejects a customer at the notorious waterfront
dive, Shanghai Reds, Beacon and Fifth Streets, San Pedro, ca. 1953.

Central Avenue. Hot and always happening. The center for Negro clubs, the area around 41st Street was a West Coast version of New York's Harlem. **Top.** Central Avenue guide to businesses and clubs, ca. 1944. **Middle.** Lionel Hampton receives a celebrity welcome in front of the Club Alabam, ca. 1941. **Bottom.** Central Avenue businesses catering to the Black community mingled with nightspots along the "Avenue," ca. 1942.

South Central L.A. played host to numerous nightspots, both on and around Central Avenue. An implied sense of danger gave the area a forbidding and unlawful quality, an edge that made it the perfect setting for many noir writers. **Left.** Souvenir photo holders from various Central Avenue area clubs. **Top.** A packed Club Alabam, one of the larger Central Avenue clubs, ca. 1944. **Bottom.** Interior of the Cafe Society, another popular gathering spot in South Central L.A., ca. 1946.

Raids were synonymous with Black clubs. While police found illegal activity throughout L.A., nightspots in "certain" parts of town received a disproportionate amount of harassment. **Opposite.** Raid at Cafe Zombie, 5434 South Central Avenue, ca. 1947. **Top Left.** Police hassle patrons at the Cafe Society, 2711 South San Pedro Street, eventually arresting thirty-eight persons, ca. 1947. **Top Right.** Confiscated booze at a Central Avenue nightclub, ca. 1949. **Bottom.** White and Black patrons get rousted at the Casablanca Club, 2801 South San Pedro Street, in a sweeping "purify Los Angeles" drive, ca. 1950.

The Hollywood Legion Stadium, behind the Vine Street Derby on El Centro Avenue, played host to the area's major boxing matches. A favorite pastime for movie stars, sporting events attracted more than their share of underworld characters and under-the-table deals.

The Olympic Auditorium in downtown Los Angeles was a grittier venue for sportive pleasures and replaced the Vernon Arena in 1925 with seating for 15,000. It, too, had a reputation for harboring a criminal element in its cigar-soaked halls.

KOOKS, CRAZIES & REDEMPTION

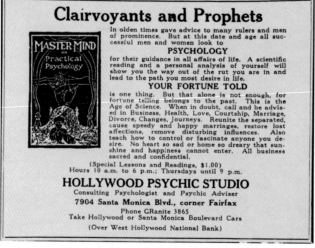

Clairvoyants and seers found Hollywood and Los Angeles the answer to their prayers. Hordes of lost souls sought their counsel at temples and psychic studios, blindly following oriental rites, breathing exercises, and endless gimmick cures for all that ailed them. **Opposite.** Posed at a Hollywood stage show, an eastern mystic awaits his following, ca. 1933. **Above.** Frank Ormsby points out his Pyramid Cube University in Alhambra, where participants could plot the planets and figure out the future, ca. 1932.

A barefoot fitness faddist greets a female customer at his Hollywood health food restaurant, ca. 1935.

Dance marathons masqueraded as entertainment for a fad-hungry Los Angeles whose population gobbled up the sport. The Depression-era craze served as the background for *They Shoot Horses Don't They?*, a novel set in a seaside ballroom similar to the one advertised in this brochure.

Pet cemeteries and the rituals of death fascinated visitors and writers alike, who found these types of establishments just another of the region's bizarre cultural aberrations.

91

Top. In the hills above L.A. an odd assortment of characters pursued their passions. The Palestine Exhibit brought the Middle East to the Edendale section of Los Angeles. Created by "Golden Ark Explorer" A. F. Futterer, it was advertised as "A Trip Through the Bible World in a Day." Costumed tour guides led the uninitiated through an Arab village with goat hair tents and an Egyptian mummy. Visitors had access to King Tut's parlor on the top floor and were treated to refreshments while seated on a Persian carpet. **Bottom.** Nudist colonies flourished in the counties east of L.A. Olympic Fields near Lake Elsinore further supported the notion that Southern Californians were uninhibited free spirits unencumbered by convention.

Top. A Hollywood fixture, this newspaper vendor may have inspired Nathaneal West's character, Abe Kusich, the loud-mouthed dwarf and bookie who lived at the fictional San Berdoo Arms apartments. **Bottom.** Kooks and nut cases found Hollywood Boulevard a hospitable environment. Here a sandal- and sackcloth-garbed Hollywood aesthete rests along the street.

Peter the Hermit, a long-term Hollywood character, fulfilled every stereotype of the Hollywood "nut." Pictured here in a publicity pose, he lived in a tent in the nearby hills. He fancied himself as a guru, lived off the land, and drove around in a goat cart. Dressed in tattered clothes, he ventured down to the Boulevard, walking staff in hand, for long-winded conversations with tourists and locals, reaping celebrity status and healthy doses of publicity.

L.A.'s most famous evangelist, Aimee Semple McPherson shrewdly combined theatrics and admonitions to her needy followers to "Give, give, give until it hurts! Praise the Lord." Captivating thousands of followers with elaborate shows staged at her Foursquare Church in Echo Park, pictured above, she also broadcast her sermons to thousands more who sent in contributions, keeping Sister Aimee well endowed despite several scandal-tinged episodes. If L.A. was a city poisoned by sin, Sister Aimee was its antidote.

The Reverend "Bob" Shuler, pastor of Trinity Methodist Church in downtown L.A., was Sister Aimee's main competition in the soul-saving business. The reverend proved also to be a tireless fire-and-brimstone critic of the corrupt political machine that ran L.A. Issuing tracts and publications, he openly condemned public officials, exposed graft, and even landed himself in jail for being too much of a "rabble rouser."

RROR MURDER

opolitan

No. 16,223

MOND 6565

ee up

avy -long ow

Jan. 16.
nd Navy
agreement
an, it was
and Presi-
recommend
ed legisla-
-equal air
all three
ngle secre-
ense.

more than
inter-service
avy leaders,
Navy James
up solidly

House an-
accord was
rrestal and
ert P. Pat-
to Truman
mmendations
n required.
secretary
full details
n would be
al press con-
morrow, at

VICTIM OF A CRAZED FIEND
Elizabeth Short, 22, was tortured and butchered

—Acme telephoto.

Talmadge in driver's seat, but Arnall still fighting

ATLANTA, Ga., Jan. 16.-UP-An explosion and tear-gas, apparently the work of pranksters, punctuated Georgia's dual governorship
crisis today as Gov. Herman Talmadge seized the gubernatorial offices
and the executive mansion and posted state police to keep Gov. Ellis
Arnall out.

The explosion, climaxing a fan-
tastic day in the statehouse, was
touched off on a balcony over-
looking Arnall's emergency desk
in the Capitol rotunda. Investigation revealed that it came from

AFL raiders beat up 12

Identify victim as Hollywood resident

(Additional story on Page 3)

A definite suspect has been
established in the brutal murder of 22-year-old Elizabeth
Short, whose mutilated body
was found dumped in a va-
cant lot in southwestern Los
Angeles Wednesday morning.

Identification of the girl was
made last night by police from
copies of her fingerprints on file
with the FBI in Washington.

Elizabeth was a Massachusetts
girl who recently lived at a hotel
at 1611 N. Orange Dr., in Hollywood.

In 1943 she was a civilian em-
ploye at a post exchange at Camp
Cooke, near Lompoc, and more
recently worked at the naval hos-
pital in San Diego.

Investigators, who said they
were withholding the name of the
suspect for the present, declared
that he might be the man of
whom Elizabeth told friends she
was "deadly afraid."

That Elizabeth lived in fear of
a suitor was substantiated in San
Diego by Mrs. Vera French and
her daughter, Dorothy.

The Frenchs, who live at 2750
Camino Tadaro, Pacific Beach,
said Elizabeth lived with them
from last Dec. 12 until Jan. 8,
when she hurriedly left for Hollywood.

Mrs. French told officers that
Elizabeth, whom she had met in
San Diego, was very popular with
men and had many dates. The
girl, she said, often spoke, however, about a boy friend from
whom she was always hiding because of an unexplained fear.

Harold Frank Costa, 31, and
Donald Leyes, 22, who lived in
the same Hollywood hotel last

Daily News **3**
LOS ANGELES, CALIFORNIA
WEDNESDAY, JANUARY 22, 1947

Boddy meets new kind of pioneers

By MANCHESTER BODDY
(Publisher of the Daily News)

BERLIN, Jan. 21.-(Special)
Today, quite by accident, I
met two pioneers. Not throw-
backs to the old school I used
to worship as a youngster. In
those days I thought all pioneers were Westerners who
fought Indians, built log
houses, and civilized wild
country.

The pioneers I met today are
tumbleweeds caught in the strong
winds that are blowing the people
of the earth into the big corral we
call "one world." They didn't look
like pioneers; just a couple of
kids, as a matter of fact—an
American boy who married an
English girl.

They were searching for a billet
and had dropped over to inquire
about when we might be moving
out. They seemed so young and
inexperienced that I thought I
should fill them in with what I
knew about living in Berlin.

"Ever been here before?" I
asked.

"Oh yes," John (as we will call
him) said. "I was here in 1943."

"But that was when the Ger-
mans were very much on top."

"Yes," he said, in a matter of
fact way. "That's when I came
here. I was a bomber. Just about
over this house as a matter of fact
when I parachuted."

(Continued on Page 34, Col. 1)

McNarney in move to aid German trade

BERLIN, Jan. 21.-UP-Gen. Jo-
seph T. McNarney recommended
today, as a major step to restore
German economy, that the United
States repeal the Trading With
the Enemy Act and remove German firms in many foreign na-

rived
e girl
en in

orted
abeth
were
illiam

1 oft-
fre-
saw
part

body
olice-
g the
dark-
ection
reat-

Mc-
ators
1 had
4)

rough
n land

roject
the

WHAT HAPPENED IN APARTMENT 501!

IN HOLLYWOOD, where strange things happen
with regularity, a group of lovely, vivacious
women shared an apartment—Apartment 501—
at 1842 N. Cherokee Ave. One of those women
was Elizabeth (Beth) Short, known as "The Black
Dahlia." Pictured here with her are some of
her many female companions.

VELMA GORDON
ed in "Dahlia's" album

LYNN MARTIN
Held for questioning

TONI SMITH
nts to help police

ANN TOTH
She shared apartment

Opposite. With cotton plugs filling
gunshot wounds, Benjamin "Bugsy"
Siegel awaits the coroner, ca. 1947.

HEADLINE CRIME

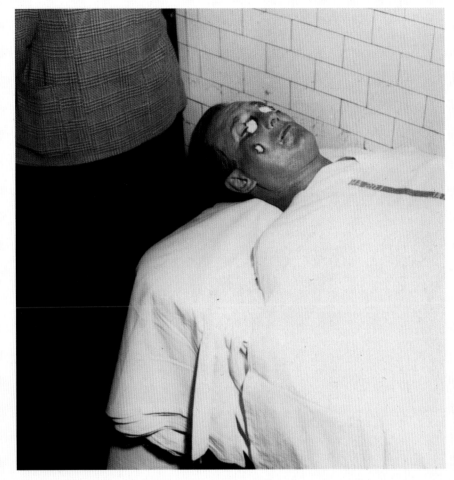

April 13, 1924, in the foothills near San Fernando, detectives discover the body of Dr. Benjamin Baldwin stuffed in a trunk after being shot in the back of the head by Mrs. Margaret Willis. Willis, who walked into the Detective Bureau the day after the murder, calmly stated, "I've killed a man. I want to tell you about it." The man she had killed was Dr. Baldwin. Married three times and known for his "wanderlust," the doctor was shot after he attacked her, Margaret said. Detectives discovered otherwise. Maragaret, a widow and steel-willed realtor, had money problems. Margaret also had a hobby. A devotee of "new science," she had toyed with harnessing ether waves. Under questioning she proclaimed, "I have studied science. I have learned that human life is no more than the life of an animal." Apparently so. A relationship gone awry was suspected for Mrs. Willis's shooting Dr. Baldwin. After stuffing his body in a trunk she had delivered to her apartment the previous day, she stored him in her room for twenty-four hours. Then with the help of a neighbor, they drove around the Southland searching for a perfect dumping spot, settling for the embankment in the Valley.

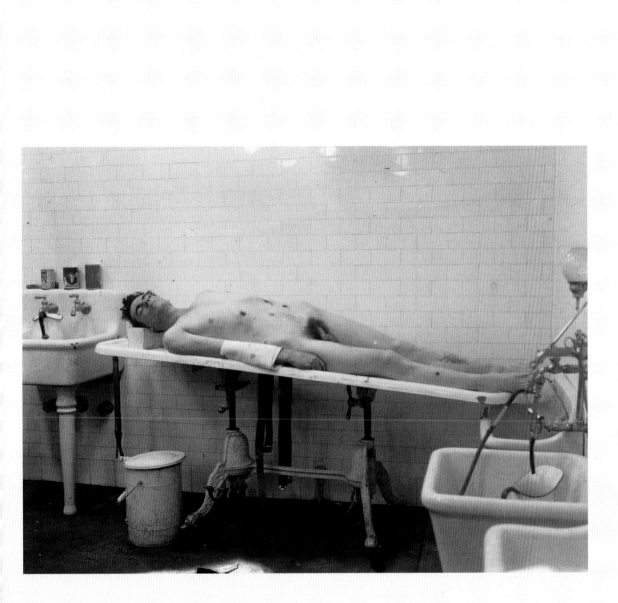

Jack Hawkins, on the coroner's slab, January 21, 1929. The tale of John Hawkins and fellow convict "Zeke" Hayes was one of a long line of suspicious killings by L.A. law enforcers. The pair, accused of kidnapping, shooting, and leaving a San Francisco cop chained to a pillar to die, were brought to L.A. County Jail to be tried. Having just appeared at a hearing regarding a continuance on their cases at the Hall of Justice, the two were escorted by sheriff's deputies into an elevator where a handcuffed Hawkins produced a gun. A shoot-out ensued and Hawkins was promptly shot five times by Deputy Sheriff "Casey" Jones. An investigation revealed inconsistencies and questionable police activities. The Rev. "Bob" Shuler, a popular local evangelist straight out of the Bible Belt, smelled a rat, and said so on his radio program. He suggested his sources had found that Hawkins had been supplied with the gun and set up by Jones so that Jack, the cop-killer, would receive immediate justice—Sheriff's Department style. Jones sued for slander, charges were dismissed and L.A. justice continued on its merry way.

Edward Hickman, psychopathic child murderer. Edward Hickman was a disturbed, diminutive nineteen-year-old when he kidnapped and dismembered a twelve-year-old school girl named Marion Parker. It was December of 1927 when Hickman abducted the daughter of a mid-Wilshire bank executive and phoned the father for ransom. After several days Hickman panicked, strangled the girl and dismembered her, leaving various limbs scattered throughout Elysian Park. Still intent on the ransom, he arranged a pick-up location. To assure the father the child was alive he offered to drive by with her in the car. Propping up the torso on a crate and wiring the corpse's eyelids open, he covered her head with a blanket and drove by the father, received the money, and slid the body onto the sidewalk a block away. Escaping Los Angeles, he was apprehended in Oregon and brought back to be tried for murder. In one of the first cases to use the by-reason-of-insanity plea, Hickman was also subjected to a courtroom inspection of his skin. The theory advanced at the time was that if the skin was scratched and the marks turned red, it was a sure indicator of guilt. The sensational trial photos, including the remains of the child, cinched Hickman's sentence. He was found guilty and was hanged for one of the city's more gruesome murders.

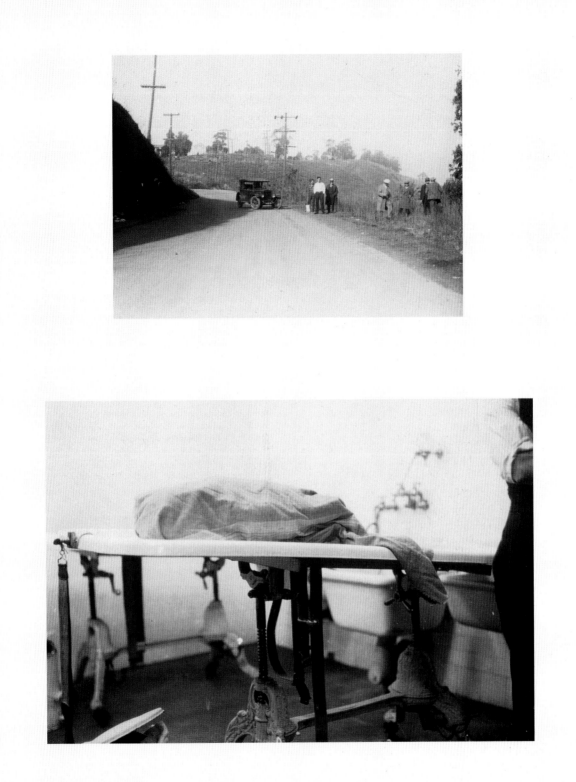

Top. Detectives recover Marion Parker's body parts dropped throughout Elysian Park.
Bottom. The wrapped torso of twelve-year-old Marion Parker in the morgue.

Thelma Todd's Joyas restaurant on Roosevelt Highway near Malibu. The "Ice Cream Blonde," Todd's nickname around town, was suspected of being murdered after a Saturday night party at the Trocadero where she was seen having a spat with ex-husband and agent, Pat DeCicco. But several witnesses claimed to have seen and spoken with her the following day, twelve hours after police officials claimed she had died. At the beachside restaurant that bore her name, Thelma's partner and sometimes paramour, director Roland West, claimed to have heard Thelma come home that night after the Troc party. But he had bolted the door to the apartments they shared above the restaurant, forcing Thelma to climb the stairs to her car parked in a garage on the street above. Or so he said. He didn't bother to check in on her that Sunday. The following Monday Todd's maid found Thelma dead in the car, still dressed in her gown and fur, with throat abrasions. The coroner said she died of carbon monoxide poisoning. A suicide. But why had Thelma confided in friends that she was being followed and was in mortal fear weeks before her death? And what about the extortion notes she had been receiving? And those half a dozen witnesses who had heard from or seen Thelma that Sunday? None of it added up. Thelma's attorney conjectured that underworld elements had snuffed Thelma after she refused to capitulate to their demands to open a gambling den above the restaurant. Others fingered DeCicco or West as the suspects. The cops and the district attorney, said to have been pressured by outside sources, eventually sidestepped the investigation, and Thelma's death remains a mystery.

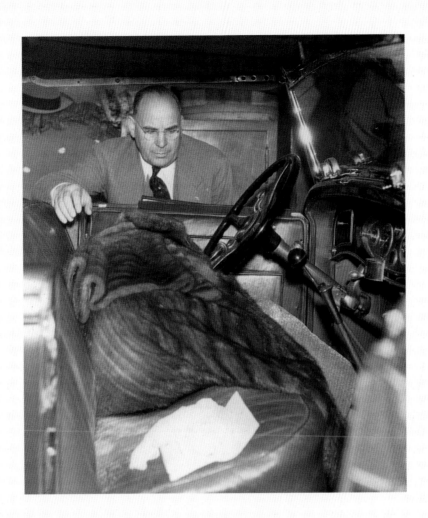

Top. A lifeless fur-clad Thelma Todd as detective Bert Wallis found her, slumped on the seat of her car, December 16, 1935. **Bottom.** Crowds view the body of Thelma Todd before services at Wee Kirk O' the Heather in Forest Lawn.

Robert James, the "Rattlesnake Murderer," July 1936. He slid into L.A. in 1934 leaving behind him a trail of pregnant girls, ex-wives, and a dead spouse. Winona, his third wife, mysteriously died in Colorado, leaving Robert a $14,000 double indemnity settlement. This unexpected cash flow, in the midst of the Great Depression, allowed James to move west and open a barbershop in downtown L.A. at 8th Street and Olive. He brought his niece with him, introducing her as his wife, and set her up as a manicurist in his shop. Robert soon fell for another female and married her. When she declined to get an insurance policy after their marriage, he insisted on annulling the union. While awaiting the annulment, he met and married an attractive twenty-five-year-old named Mary Busch. They rented a house in the foothill community of La Cañada. After they moved in, neighbors reported hearing tortured lovemaking. Not surprisingly, Mary, with a $10,000 insurance policy taken out for her just after their marriage, was soon found dead. Coroners claimed she was the victim of an accidental drowning in James's backyard fish pond. Insurance investigators found out differently. A twisted tale of incest, leather whips, and rattlesnakes emerged. Robert, it seems, once again needed easy money and decided to cash in on his new bride's insurance policy. His sex life now included sadomasochistic whippings provided by a leather-clad Mary, who was pregnant. With the help of a Hermosa Beach hash slinger, he arranged to fake an abortion on their kitchen table, instead inserting her leg into a box filled with two rattlesnakes. The snakebites were slowly killing the bound and gagged newlywed, who writhed in agony for hours. This method proved too slow for James, who took the unconscious Mary and drowned her in the bathtub. Depositing her body near the fish pond, he made it look like she had grown dizzy from her pregnancy and had accidentally fallen and drowned. James and his accomplice were tried and convicted. Robert James, whose real name was Major Lisenba, was the last person to be hung in California.

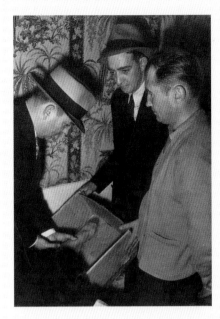

Top. Detectives re-enact how James put his wife's foot in a rattlesnake-filled box. **Bottom.** The fish pond behind the La Cañada house where Robert James drowned his wife after subjecting her to hours of torture.

Hollywood's attempt to permanently closet its homosexual populace fell apart momentarily in a sordid episode that kept assorted celebs behind closed doors for years. Former silent-film actor William Haines was one of a few openly gay stars and his career plummeted when studio heads deemed him scandal fodder. Switching careers, he operated a successful interior design business supported by friends such as Joan Crawford. In the summer of 1936, he and a group of friends rented a summer house in El Porto next to Manhattan Beach. Their antics met with disapproval by neighbors who wanted this undesirable element out of their neighborhood. On the evening of May 31, an informal mob, fueled by rumors that Haines's boyfriend Jimmie Shields had molested a six-year-old, slugged members of the group and threw tomatoes. They quickly packed and left town. Hints of Klan backing were never substantiated and morals complaints were dropped, but the incident effectively kept gay actors and actresses permanently underground. **Top.** Lovers William Haines and Jimmie Shields appear at a hearing after a Manhattan Beach mob roughed them up and chased them out of town, June 1936. **Bottom.** The rented house at 221 Moonstone Street, El Porto, where "gay" summer parties got some of Hollywood's swishier celebs in trouble.

Top. Mobster Mickey Cohen and cohorts Mike Howard, Sol Davis, and James Rist await jail time. Cohen hogged headlines for over twenty years as his exploits and dirty dealings fascinated and disgusted crime watchers. August 1948. **Bottom.** Early in his crime career, Cohen knocked off an enemy and operated a bookie joint at this unassuming false-front paint store on Beverly Boulevard.

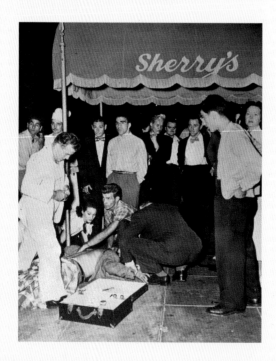

Top. A diagram points out where two hitmen hid while waiting for Mickey Cohen to leave a Sunset Strip hangout. "The Mickster" almost got rubbed out in front of Sherry's restaurant in a gangland ambush that killed his bodyguard Neddie Herbert and wounded columnist Florabell Muir. Cohen escaped untouched, July 19, 1949. **Below.** Cohen henchman Neddie Herbert is lifted into an ambulance after he was wounded in the "Battle of Sunset Strip." **Opposite Below.** Neddie Herbert lies on the sidewalk in front of Sherry's after being shot in the back by unknown assailants.

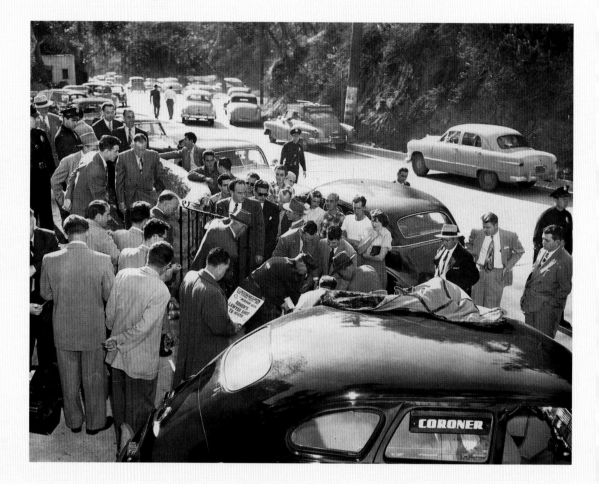

Lawyer Sammy Rummel, Mickey Cohen's mouthpiece, gets knocked off in his Laurel Canyon digs. Rummel, suspected of investing too heavily in Gardena card clubs, was believed to have been set up by Nevada gaming concerns who were muscling in on local legalized poker clubs, December 1950.

Mickey Cohen observes the remnants of another plot to kill him. Neighbors declared him "Public Nuisance Number 1" after a bomb blasted a chunk out of his Brentwood home, February 1950.

112

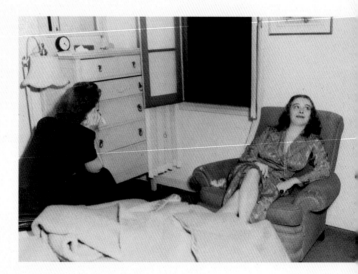

Top. Brenda Allen, Madam to the Stars, in the middle of a vice bust makes a hasty retreat from her rented brothel at 8406 Harold Way, above Sunset Strip, May 1948. **Bottom.** Dressed and ready for jail, a couple of Brenda's girls pout and display the wares that got them into trouble.

A fashionable Brenda in court with celebrity lawyer Jerry Giesler, ca. 1948.

A dapper and amicable Bugsy Siegel poses in court to answer questions concerning his employment. His smile was his answer, ca. 1940.

Bugsy sprawled on the couch of Virginia Hill's rented Beverly manse, June 20, 1947. Returning from a trout dinner in Ocean Park, Siegel and his bodyguard retired to the couch to catch the early editions of the newspapers. At 10:45 p.m. sharpshooters expertly extracted both his eyes, whacking Hollywood's most well-known mobster. Speculators figured too much money was mishandled in the construction of the Vegas Flamingo and East Coast bosses wanted him eliminated.

Robert Mitchum, convicted reefer smoker, marches from the county jail to the honor farm in Castaic California, February 1949.

After completing a fifty-day sentence, a reformed Mitchum contemplates fresh air in front of the Hall of Justice, March 1949.

Top. Police, coroners, and the press arrive at the vacant lot where the body of Elizabeth Short, the Black Dahlia, was dumped. January 15, 1947. **Bottom.** The bi-sected body of the Black Dahlia.

An intense Caryl Chessman, "The Red-Light Bandit," on trial for a series of rape and burglary charges. He became a cause célèbre for anti–death penalty activists when he was executed a decade after his arrest.

Top. Smart guy Johnny Stompanato (real name John Truppa) found himself constantly in and out of trouble with the law. Thug and bodyguard to Mickey Cohen, he's shown here with his attorney in court on vagrancy charges, October 1949. **Bottom.** Lana and Johnny making cozy. When Lana Turner hooked up with boyfriend Johnny Stompanato she inherited a hot-tempered wife beater. His ex explained in divorce court that "he used to stay out all night two or three times a week. Then he'd say, 'You oughta be happy that I come home at all. I don't take you any place because you bore me.' "

Johnny's way with women eventually led him to a porcelain slab in the morgue: The butcher knife allegedly used by fourteen-year-old Cheryl Crane, Lana's daughter, in the murder of Johnny Stompanato, April 1958.

Opposite. Hollywood party girls cover up as deputies question their intentions, ca. 1954.

VICE

Down the drain. Federal authorities dispose of one thousand gallons of Jamaica ginger extract seized from a Los Angeles warehouse during an investigation of "ginger jake" alcohol poisoning, ca. 1931.

Prohibition laid the foundation for L.A.'s crime-ridden future. Speakeasies prospered in the most innocent-looking establishments. **Top.** Beer was for the asking at Bernie's Delicatessen, 1551 North Vine Street, until investigators busted the place, ca. 1929. **Bottom.** Hardly a den of iniquity, the Italian Cafe on Western Avenue, one of nearly four hundred L.A. speakeasies, was cited for selling muscatel to undercover agents, ca. 1929.

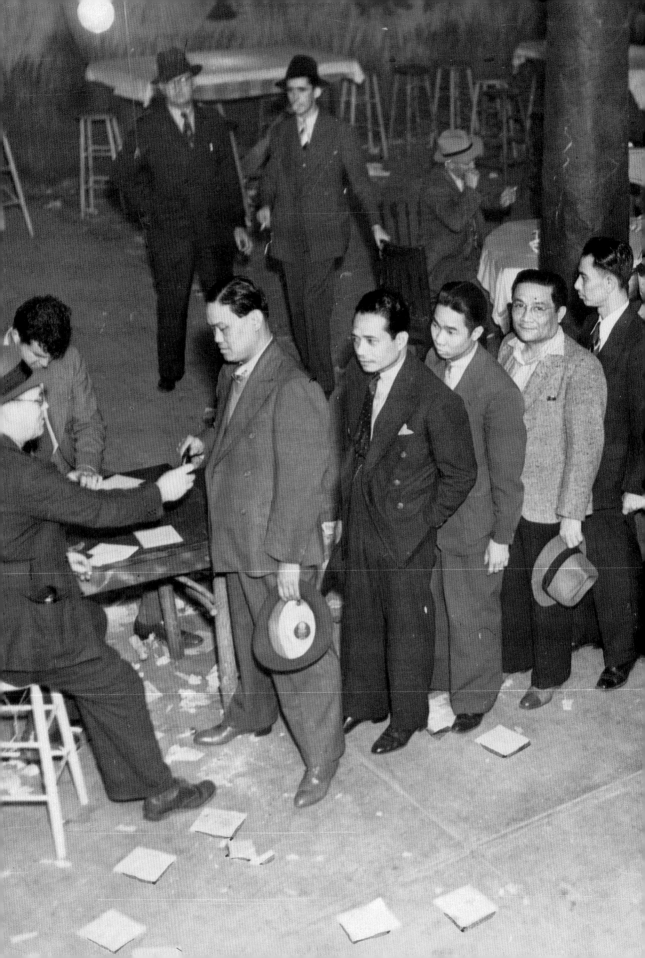

Opposite. Chinese lottery players line up for an I.D. check and "mop up" at a hastily organized gambling hall within the shadow of City Hall, ca. 1938. **Above.** A Chinatown raid nets detectives pistols, knives, "saps," and $5,000 in cash, May 25, 1938.

128

Top. A genial crook is ushered into a waiting squad car near Schwab's on the Strip, ca. 1937. **Bottom.** Bookmaking operation in full swing, ca. 1949.

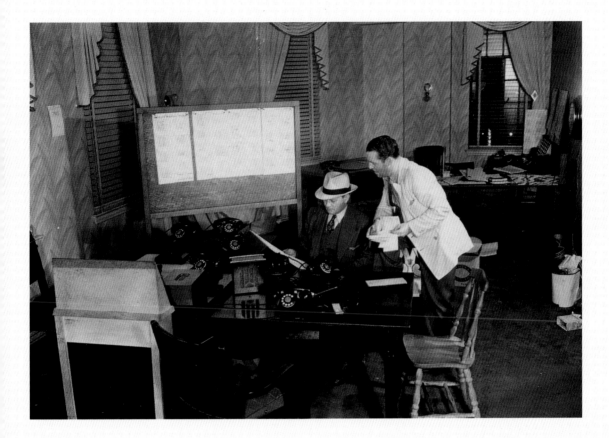

Nice set-up in classy digs. Bookie joints opened and closed with regularity depending on who was putting on the squeeze. Beverly Hills detectives examine the goods at a live one, ca. 1938.

Top. The *Rex*, Santa Monica Bay's most renowned gambling ship, awaits the Sheriff's Department men approaching the barge for a raid, ca. 1938. **Bottom.** The operation. Gaming tables and slot machines gleam, ready for the evening's "squirrels" to arrive.

"The Royal Crown seemed to ride as steady as a pier on its four hausers. Its landing stage was lit up like a theater marquee. Then all this faded into remoteness and another, older smaller boat began to sneak out into the night towards us. It was not much to look at. A converted sea-going freighter with scummed and rusted plates, the superstructure cut down to the boatdeck level, and above that two stumpy masts just high enough for a radio antenna. There was a light on the *Montecito* also, and music floated across the wet dark sea." *Farewell, My Lovely*, Raymond Chandler

Cops and Robbers. Another raid on the *Rex* with owner and operator, Tony Cornero (on the left) showing off his playing equipment to Johnny Klein, D.A. investigator; George Contreras, Captain of the Sheriff's Department; and Charles Dice, Chief of the Santa Monica Police, May 1936.

Top. Aboard the *Rex*, cops detain patrons while the ship gets the once-over, ca. 1939. **Bottom.** Slot machines from the gambling ship *Lux* are given the heave-ho onto a waiting barge for the trip back to the mainland, February 1941. **Opposite.** The *Rex* under assault. During the "Battle of Santa Monica Bay," Tony Cornero's "associates" keep the Sheriff's Department at bay by hosing their speedboats, August 1939.

Officer J. K. Harvey inspects a marijuana hoard seized in a hotel room. The suitcase of weed was valued at $10,000, October 1945.

The film colony loved its reefer. Here dapper Detective Sergeants Rappatoni and Duede test marijuana taken as evidence in a raid at the fashionable apartment of a starlet and a stunt man, March 1945.

Marijuana plants, and a conveniently placed poster, are displayed in the precinct station for full publicity value, ca. 1946.

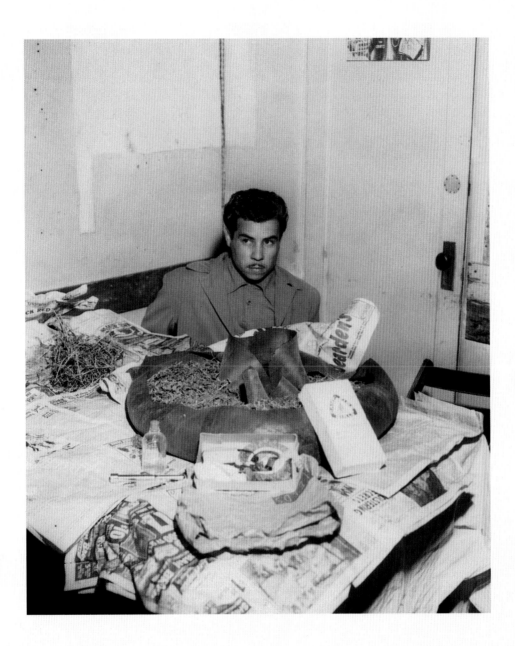

A "reefer man" gets an impromptu mug shot behind stacks of his stash, ca. 1952.

Bundles of pills get the once-over by Captain Kearney back at the station, ca. 1943.

Investigators pore over a narcotics haul. L.A.'s proximity to the Mexican border made it a prime destination for a variety of illegal substances, ca. 1948.

Top. Fortified casino at 182nd Street and Western Avenue. Around the resort was a high fence screening activities from the street. Officers said it was the most pretentious gambling layout they had ever seen, ca. 1938. **Bottom.** Post-raid interior of a typical illegal gaming joint in L.A., ca. 1947.

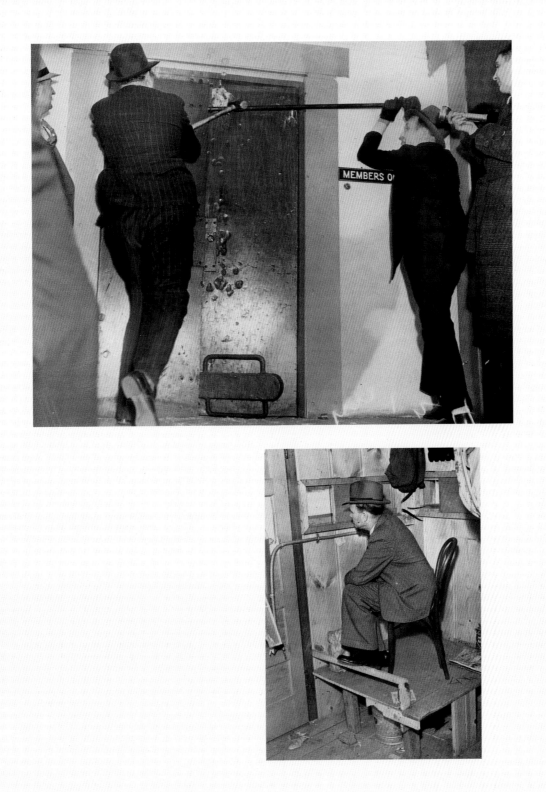

Top. Raid at gambling compound, 182nd and Western Avenue. The raiders crashed through the gate, then battered their way into the elaborately furnished casino amid a fusillade of bullets. Raiders seized $18,000 in cash, arrested eleven Chinese, and sent "two hundred Negro patrons scrambling wildly," ca. 1938. **Bottom**. Patrons of gambling tables in makeshift casinos had to pass the scrutiny of a peephole guard who occupied this station. Captain Hunter demonstrates the procedure, November 1938.

Finding a loophole in a 1938 law that allowed draw poker to be played legally on a local-option basis in California, L.A.'s criminal element quickly established card clubs outside L.A. city limits. The city of Gardena welcomed the tax revenue and soon several clubs were raking in a lucrative business. **Top.** Plain and fancy. Smartly dressed floor girls wait on customers in less than luxurious environs. The Monterey Club, ca. 1938. **Bottom.** A floor girl gets chips from a cashier for customers at a legalized poker hall in Gardena, ca. 1938.

A trio of Gardena card clubs, part of the legalized gambling that flourished in the post-war Southland. **Top.** The Gardena Club. **Middle.** The Monterey Club. **Bottom.** The Normandie Club, all ca. 1949.

Jade and Tango parlors were another form of legalized gambling spawned by underworld figures to bypass the law. These thinly veiled skill games were set up to the house advantage, but come-ons such as free food and spiffy surroundings kept the parlors filled. The Jade Tango Parlor on West Adams Boulevard, ca. 1932.

The interior of the Monterey Club in Gardena, the first of the legal draw poker clubs in the city, ca. 1940.

The Venice Pier pulled in crowds of revelers looking for inexpensive excitement.
Writers of the noir found it the perfect locale for fog-shrouded intrigue, ca. 1940.

Top. Another front for penny-ante crime, mechanical horse races were shut down when investigators exposed their fixed winnings. **Bottom.** Bridgo parlors with exotic names such as Cameo, Vogue, Shamrock, and Canasto were a variation of the same old con game that kept popping up in beachfront amusement zones. The "sucker games" were wiped out in Venice in a clampdown of the racket in 1949.

Members of the LAPD vice squad check out a pile of confiscated smut in a porno ring bust.

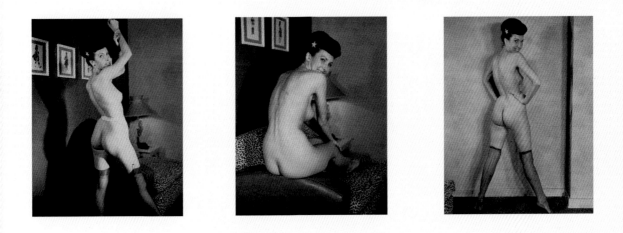

High-class girlie shots, the bread and butter of "art" photographers, brought in bundles of dough and exploited starlets-in-the-making.

Chasing "prosties" could be dangerous business. An undercover vice dick holds a three-inch knife retrieved from the prostitute who slashed him above the right eye, ca. 1957.

A vice squad raid at the Carolina Pines Restaurant on Melrose Avenue nets a bevy of hookers, ca. 1957.

Firmly entrenched underground, the homosexual community in Hollywood occasionally showed its colors. Jimmy's Backyard on Ivar, which opened in 1929, was the first openly gay nightclub in Hollywood. **Top.** Joining it was the Barn, on Cahuenga Avenue just below Sunset, which, according to newspapers, "featured a floor show in which men masqueraded as women and women posed as men." Continuing their drive against "certain types" of Hollywood nightclubs, the vice squad shut down many in 1933. **Bottom.** A typical drag show in the sparse surroundings of a "Hollywood degenerate" hangout, ca. 1947.

A drag queen chanteuse with piano accompaniment graces another Hollywood twilight club, ca. 1940.

154

18th ANNUAL
BAL MASQUE
"DRAG BALL"
PRESENTED
Hallowe'en—Oct. 31, 1949

PRICE
50c
Souvenir

Promoter Bill Heflin threw his first drag ball at Dreamland at Fourth Street and Central Avenue, followed by other affairs at the Humming Bird Black and Tan Cafe, the Plantation, the Morocco, Red Apple, and the Saw Dust Trail, all in South Central L.A. **Top.** This one at the Club Alabam, in the heart of Central Avenue, was billed as the eighteenth, ca. 1949. **Bottom.** Program cover for 1949 Bal Masque "drag ball" featured "Betty Boops," queen of the 1948 ball.

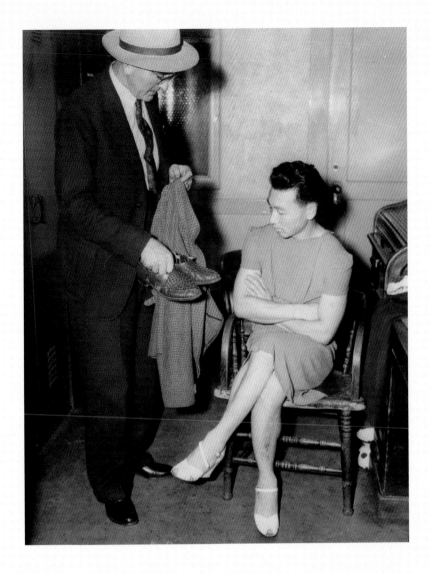

A cross-dresser is handed "regular" clothes after being picked up on morals charges, ca. 1945.

NOIR WRITERS

L.A.'s dark side inspired a group of writers whose close-up visions of a dream gone awry were instrumental in creating the image of this city's dark underbelly. The glaring sunshine, dull blocks of bungalows and tract houses, the slums of Bunker Hill, and the city's east side provided fodder for these scribes. Few of these writers were natives. Authors such as Raymond Chandler, Nathanael West, John Fante, Evelyn Waugh, and Aldous Huxley drew inspiration from local news accounts. The tales were there for the asking. The local rags and newspapers published the city's dirtiest laundry. Digging for stories about the sullen side of the Southland was like shooting fish in a barrel. Avoiding the simplicity of rearranging tabloid headlines, early writers of the noir culled these stories, adding the chaos and cynicism of the corrupt city, and drafted their observations into murky visions of a not-so-pretty paradise. The results were the stories, the novels, and films of the noir.

Later, a new crop of writers such as John Gregory Dunne, Walter Mosley, and James Ellroy tapped into the same vein. Like their predecessors, they filled pages with average housewives gone bad, two-bit body guards, sinister sanitariums, bloated bodies, rotting corpses, and syphilitic whores. From the dreams and nightmares of the real city they crafted fact into fiction, and the photographs substantiated their writings.

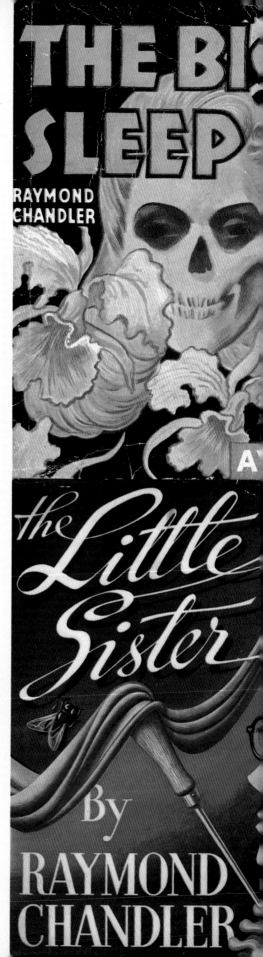

L.A. AND THE NOIR FILM

Los Angeles was the favored city of images for American film noir. The city lent itself to cinematic exploitation. It provided cinematographers with a feast of locations and images they could make look like heaven—or hell—on earth. The wet, blurred city streets, the vacuous concrete of the Los Angeles River bed, the fading slums of Bunker Hill were woven into films such as *Sunset Boulevard*, *He Walked by Night*, and *Kiss Me Deadly*. In *Touch of Evil* a moody Venice, California, even stood in for Tijuana. Los Angeles provided the darkness, alienation, and irony that were hallmarks of the noir world.

" 'Give me the money.' The motor of the grey Plymouth throbbed under her voice and the rain pounded above it. The violet light at the top of Bullock's green-tinged tower was far above us, serene and withdrawn from the dark, dripping city."

The Big Sleep, Raymond Chandler

Bullock's Wilshire, ca. 1933.

THE PHOTOGRAPHERS

Early in the twentieth century, the city was filled with daily tabloids: the *Los Angeles Times*, the *Daily News*, the *Mirror*, the *Examiner*, the *Herald,* the *Hollywood Citizen*. Photographers such as Delmar Watson represented the typical news photographer. George Watson, Delmar's uncle, worked initially for the *Times*, later becoming manager of Pacific and Atlantic Photos, a forerunner of United Press International Wire Photos. One of the town's most aggressive news photographers, George Watson shot the region's most acclaimed personalities, events, disasters, and crimes. Delmar Watson described the Los Angeles shooting scene as one that was free form and filled with spontaneous decision making. Bruce Henstell in his book *Sunshine and Wealth* quotes *Daily News* editor Matt Weinstocks describing his newspaper's staff of ten photographers as uncontrollable: they "could terrorize everyone with flash powder which after the explosion filled the vicinity with throat-searing smoke."

After the war and into the fifties, stringers for East Coast scandal sheets such as *Confidential* shot viciously unflattering celeb shots, or anything that looked like a story. Forerunners of today's paparazzi, they were an unorganized group who were an unwelcome intrusion around town.

A few commercial photographers, in the course of their assignments, caught another side of the Southland: the posed and precise Los Angeles. The Mott, Dick Whittington, Merge, and other studios produced some of the most enduring images of L.A. A studied treatment was given to tourist attractions, architecture, movie premieres, grocery store openings, flossed-up streets, and hand shaking politicians. Together with the freewheeling newspaper photographers, they captured the genuine Los Angeles noir.

NOTE ON THE PHOTOGRAPHS

Many of the photographs that appear in this book were culled from archives and special collections that have become depositories for newspaper "morgues," the equivalent of an in-house photo library. Their quality reflects the original use. Retouching, crop marks, and low-grade paper reveal the "quick and dirty" nature of photographs intended for immediate publication. Age has deteriorated some of the emulsion, while some show cracks from storage. Few retain the physical quality of what could be called art prints. Prints from commercial photographers, on the other hand, are almost always accompanied by original negatives. The negatives were usually catalogued for future client use and prints made from these good negs are generally pristine. While visuals captured in both studio and on-the-spot conditions differ in technical traits, the aesthetic level of the images from both sources is of indisputable gallery quality.

Top. The Whittington mobile truck covers a race at Santa Anita. Such elaborate equipment set his studio apart from other local commercial photographers. **Bottom.** The newsroom at the *Hollywood Citizen* shows photographer Cliff Wesselman amidst the stuff of a quick paced tabloid. **Opposite.** Mickey Cohen, outside his Sunset Boulevard haberdashery, examines the spot where an associate was shot during an attempt on his life.

BIBLIOGRAPHY

Anderson, Clinton. *Beverly Hills Is My Beat.* Englewood Cliffs, New Jersey: Prentice Hall, 1960.

Cohen, Mickey. *Mickey Cohen: In My Own Words. As Told to John Peer Nugent.* Englewood Cliffs, New Jersey: Prentice Hall, 1975.

Cox, Bette Yarborough. *Central Avenue—Its Rise and Fall.* Los Angeles: BEEM Press, 1996.

Edmonds, Andy. *Hot Toddy: The True Story of Hollywood's Most Sensational Murder.* New York: William Morrow and Company, Inc., 1989.

Gillmore, John. *Severed: The Real Story of the Black Dahlia Murder.* Los Angeles: Zanja Press, 1994.

Henstell, Bruce. *Sunshine and Wealth.* San Francisco: Chronicle Books, 1982.

"How the Sex Queen of Hollywood Nearly Brought Down City Hall," *Los Angeles Magazine,* June, 1978, 70–84.

Lamparski, Richard. *Lamparski's Hidden Hollywood.* New York: Simon and Schuster, 1981.

Morrow, Mayo. *Los Angeles: A History with Side-Shows.* New York: Alfred A. Knopf, 1932.

Silver, Alain and Elizabeth Ward. *Film Noir.* Woodstock, New York: The Overlook Press, 1979.

Stoker, Charles. *Thicker'n Thieves.* Santa Monica, Calif.: Sidereal Company, 1951.

Thorpe, Edward. *Chandlertown.* New York: St. Martin's Press, 1983.

Ward, Elizabeth, and Alain Silver. *Raymond Chandler's Los Angeles.* Woodstock, New York: The Overlook Press, 1987.

Weinstock, Matt. *My L.A.* New York: Current Books, 1947.

Wolf, Marvin J., and Katherine Mader. *Fallen Angels.* New York: Facts On File Publications, 1986.

Wolsley, Serge. *Call House Madam.* New York: The Martin Tudordale Corporation, 1942.

Woon, Basil. *Incredible Land.* New York: Liveright Publishing Corporation, 1933.

Zion, Sidney. *Loyalty and Betrayal: The Story of the American Mob.* San Francisco: Collins Publishers, 1994.

159

PHOTO CREDITS